AN EDENDALE LOCAL PREPARED for the return run into Los Angeles from the Glendale Line tracks at Semi-Tropical Park, about 1907.

A MOUNT LOWE CAR waited for inbound passengers at the Rubio Canyon storage tracks above Altadena, October 23, 1907.

SOUTHERN CALIFORNIA
AND THE
PACIFIC ELECTRIC
VOLUME I

AN ALBUM BY

DANNY HOWARD

CONTENTS

SOUTHERN CALIFORNIA
AND THE
PACIFIC ELECTRIC
VOLUME I

PUBLISHED BY DANIEL L. HOWARD
LOS ANGELES, CA

PRINTED BY J & R LITHOGRAPHY
LOS ANGELES, CA

ISBN 0-936144-00-9

IN SEPTEMBER 1911 THE SOUTHERN PACIFIC bought control of eight electric rail companies, including the Pacific Electric, in what was called the Great Merger. Shortly thereafter survey crews remapped the new system. Here a survey crew is running elevation grades at Longfellow Avenue in Hermosa Beach, then a quiet residential town of 800 people.

DANNY HOWARD COLLECTION

FOREWORD

The face of Southern California had changed dramatically from the ranchero days of earlier years, when the City of the Angels became the capital of California, gold was discovered in Placerita Canyon north of San Fernando Mission, and General John C. Fremont and Army Scout Kit Carson battled through the hills to subdue belligerent factions, as agents for the Republic of California. Thousands migrated to the southland when the transcontinental railroad was linked to the area in 1878. Settlers were further enticed to the west when rate wars between the Southern Pacific and Santa Fe railroads plummeted fares from the midwest. From the mid 1880's residents of the major cities—Los Angeles, Long Beach, Pasadena, Redondo Beach, and Santa Monica—had been served with a variety of transit lines, powered by cables, electricity, steam, or horsepower. No less than 72 separately owned electric trolley companies sprang up, in and around Los Angeles prior to the turn of the century. Henry Huntington, who chummed around with Leland Stanford and Edward L. Doheny, spent some time in the southland surveying his prospects for a business venture. Stanford went north and built a notable university at Palo Alto; Doheny discovered oil and developed wells around Los Angeles; while Huntington, with some $20,000,000 to invest, developed real estate and rapid transit in the southland. Huntington began his railway empire in 1898 by acquiring the Los Angeles Railway Company, a narrow gauge yellow car line, and built it into a great system. The Pacific Electric was franchised in 1901 and from its headquarters in downtown Los Angeles expanded throughout the southland. As fast as new lines were opened, they were overwhelmed with traffic. Although a loaf of bread cost about four cents at the bakery and a gallon of milk about eight cents at the dairy, perhaps the best deal in town was a ride on the trolley cars. Fare was usually just a little more than a penny a mile. The residents of some communities sometimes paid the Pacific Electric a bonus to extend the electrified rail lines into their area. Huntington's Pacific Electric and several other electric railway companies were purchased by the Southern Pacific in 1911 in the Great Merger. The Southern Pacific continued to improve upon the company and, in keeping with the changing times, instituted the systems first motor coach service in 1917. Bigger, faster, and safer rail equipment was introduced and helped account for record traffic in the twenties. Notwithstanding the pressure to motorize its public transportation services, the company proposed a bond issue in both 1917 and 1927 to pay for the public cost of an extensive rapid transit system using the Pacific Electric's already existing network of rail lines. Both issues were defeated. A short but very useful subway was opened in downtown Los Angeles in 1926. California's first freeway was opened in 1939 between Los Angeles and Pasadena which attested to the growing popularity of the automobile. Pacific Electric passenger equipment slowly depreciated from a lack of public support; however, in 1937 the company handled over 102,000 freight cars which rated as third highest of all California carriers. The Rehabilitation Program of 1939–41 further stimulated bus operations as a substitute for unprofitable rail lines. Gasoline, oil, steel, and rubber quotas restricted the use of motor vehicles during World War II and brought about the unprecedented demand on the rail system. Both passenger and freight records were broken. The post war boom continued to escalate freight business while passenger traffic continued to decline. New freeways soon paralleled many of the Pacific Electric's rapid transit lines, and the demise of the great system as a public carrier was eminent. Passenger service was sold to the Metropolitan Coach Lines in 1953 and subsequently to the Metropolitan Transit Authority in 1958 in a last ditch effort to maintain effective rail service. This failed and service was discontinued April 9, 1961. Freight operations were consolidated with the Southern Pacific in August, 1965. Today much of the system's right of way is still intact. Many of the rails and ties, some placed in service as long as 80 years ago, lie buried but a few inches under the asphalt cover of the city streets, or exposed, weathering in the sun and soil.

EARLY DAYS

Proclaimed "The Greatest Electric Railway System on Earth" as early as 1904, the Pacific Electric did, in fact, live up to its claim. The system operated more cars on more tracks and carried more passengers and freight than any other interurban line in the world. The early days of the company were marked with the rapid expansion of the electrified rail system throughout the southland. Laying tracks with only minimal grading, construction crews raced from town to town building culverts and trestles and installing poles, wire, ties and tracks. Within a few years Southern California was laced with a network of high speed rail lines traveled upon by more than 400 plush rail cars—every coastal city from Santa Monica Canyon to Newport Bay were connected with the inland from San Fernando and Owensmouth to San Bernardino, Riverside, and Corona.

THE PACIFIC ELECTRIC'S FIRST SHOPS, storage yards, and car houses were located at Seventh Street and Central Avenue about a mile from the heart of Los Angeles and close to the system's Northern and Southern Divisions' trunk lines. Up to 170 cars could be stored in the yards and car barn which served the system from 1902 to 1918. Every service necessary to the complete maintenance and repair of the company's property was performed at the shops, including metal stamping, welding, carpentry, upholstering, painting, wiring, etc. The subsequent growth of the rail system and the need for a large centrally located freight terminal made it necessary to relocate the shops at Torrance while the storage tracks and car houses were moved to new divisional headquarters at the Macy Street Yards. Additional equipment was relocated to facilities at Pasadena, Watts, Long Beach, and Vineyard Junction. Western Division storage yards were located at Vineyard, West Hollywood, Ocean Park, and the Hill Street Station. After the move, The Los Angeles Wholesale Terminal, its largest tenant The Union Terminal Warehouse, occupied the site.

JERRY KITTS COLLECTION

THE "BIG RED CARS," the trademark-name, aptly applied to the fleet of Pacific Electric big red rail cars, has remained the catch phrase and principal point of reference to the system. Pacific Electric Car No. 257 and another 136 of the same type formed the basis of the system's first true interurban cars. Designed by Huntington's own engineers and built by the St. Louis Car Company, the cars were delivered to Los Angeles on their own wheels in 1902. So popular were these cars that from an initial order of 20, an additional 117 were requisitioned, which constituted the largest order ever placed by an electric railway company in the world for a single class of car. The 50 foot wood, and steel cars were colored with crimson red paint and metallic gold lettering and trim. The cars were equipped with brass metal sash outside and nickled pipe railing inside. Comfortable red plush upholstered seats in a variety of modern patented styles were installed in the enclosed section while reversible wood plank seats were used in the open air section. This open air section, compatible with the local climate, was soon enclosed because of the high wind at speed, since the cars could maintain a cruising speed of 65 miles per hour. The cars were powered by four Westinghouse 75 horsepower motors. By 1911 a total of 419 passenger cars of several different classes were in service, two of which were horse drawn. After 38 years of service, Pacific Electric Car No. 257 was finally scrapped in 1940.

MARK EFFLE COLLECTION

RAY YOUNGHANS COLLECTION

A GROUP OF TRAINMEN POSED in front of the North Fair Oaks Car House in Pasadena, about 1907. Conductors and motormen, responsible for the collection of fares and the operation of the trains, were assigned into service only after breaking-in on every line on the system, and passing an examination on the operating rules and another on mechanics of the equipment. Passenger conductors and motormen were paid 25 cents per hours, with a one cent per year raise for five years, while express train conductors were paid 30 cents per hour after six months of service.

FOLLOWING PAGE: AN INBOUND LOCAL PARALLED HUNTINGTON DRIVE on the four track main line at Sierra Vista Junction located on the Alhambra-Los Angeles border in 1908. The copper trolley wire, steel span wires, cedar poles, and polished 60-pound steel rails marked the landscape when the area was mostly populated with jack rabbits, road runners, and tumbleweed. This section of track was perhaps the most heavily traveled on the entire Pacific Electric system. The outer tracks were used for local and freight traffic while the inner tracks were reserved for through and express traffic. Demand on the line was so heavy that in 1911 between 4:30 and 6:30 in the afternoon trains ran at one minute intervals to accommodate the average 23,000 passengers a day through-routed from Los Angeles to Pasadena alone. Sierra Madre, Arcadia, Monrovia, Azusa, Glendora, and other points east were reached through this Northern Division line. The Alhambra-San Gabriel Line branched to the right where another car lay over in front of the passenger station adjacent to Main Street.

CRAIG RASMUSSEN COLLECTION

RAY YOUNGHANS COLLECTION

PRECISE TIME SCHEDULES were met to ensure the continuous flow of rail traffic at the Sixth and Main Street Station. Over 1250 trains a day (not cars) made their arrival and departure on the stub end train concourse, allowing but three to five minutes for a train to get in, unload its passengers, reverse direction, and load for the outbound run. Congestion was prevalent from the station's opening in 1905, but was relieved somewhat when an elevated section was extended through the rear of the building in 1910 and to a road level connection at San Pedro Street in 1916. A huge decorative waiting room, occupied with all the necessary appurtenances–information counter, ticket office, restaurant, souvenir shop, etc.–was located inside and adjacent to the passenger loading platform. Trains were composed of from one to three cars, depending on the time of day and the general demand, and did not include local or city cars, freight, express, or specials, which sometimes consisted of four to six cars. Should a train be delayed more than five to seven minutes on its return to the station, a new train, held in reserve, was made up and placed into service, thus allowing for the continuous flow of scheduled runs. A unique electrified trough-like device, attached to the ceiling of the concourse, allowed cars to reverse their trolley poles without manual assistance. The reverse motion of the car first pushed, then pulled the pole through the Y-shaped apparatus and saved valuable seconds very necessary to the efficient operation at the station. In 1911, more than 40,000 monthly time tables were distributed for public use.

REGULARLY SCHEDULED FLYER AND EXPRESS SERVICE provided quick efficient transportation between Los Angeles and principal cities throughout the southland. Speedy flyers were usually through routed and ran nonstop to their destinations while express trains made stops only at the major points along the line. Cattle guards, milk cans, and whitewashed line poles were common landmarks at Dominguez Junction, on the Long Beach Line, where a lone passenger watched a flyer roll through, about 1907. A passenger waiting room, a 15,000 volt substation, and a control tower, operated for the safe crossover of trains at the Southern Pacific's San Pedro Branch Line, were also located at the junction. The average number of 56 trains a day was doubled on the weekend because of the heavy migration of sun bathers to the beaches. Three car trains were run every ten minutes, with every third train a flyer, to accommodate the crowds. The line was particularly conducive to high speed operations, having been built on a maximum 1% grade and having but six curves the entire distance. In the summer of 1911, flyers out of Los Angeles made the trip to Compton in 17 minutes and another 24 minutes into downtown Long Beach. In 1913, some 3,072,874 passengers rode the line. Flyer trains also operated to other important beaches on their respective lines–Newport-Balboa, Redondo, San Pedro, and Santa Monica-Venice.

CRAIG RASMUSSEN COLLECTION

HUNTINGTON LIBRARY, SAN MARINO

PEOPLE SCURRIED FOR SIDEWALK SAFETY at Sixth and Main Street where an inbound local was helped around the corner by a railway flagman standing in the center of the intersection. Pedestrian, bicycle, automobile, and horse traffic were directed by a Los Angeles peace officer. A track sweeper, who was employed to clear debris from between the rails with a broom, hitched a ride on the side steps of the car.

HUNTINGTON LIBRARY, SAN MARINO

CONCRETE CANYONS OF TOWERING SKYSCRAPERS lined Sixth Street on the Edendale Line, also used by Glendale-Burbank Line trains. A rare sight at the corner of Sixth and Broadway was the absence of a trolley car, but not many could miss the smart looking touring car, a Columbia-Knight, one of several thousand automotive types in competition with the Pacific Electric, whose eventual popularity brought about the demise of the system.

CALIFORNIA HISTORICAL SOCIETY/TITLE INSURANCE, LOS ANGELES

HOTEL
HOTEL
SOUTHERN PACIFIC PASSENGER STATION

HUNTINGTON LIBRARY, SAN MARINO

PRECEDING PAGE: THE PORT OF LOS ANGELES on the San Pedro waterfront, teemed with passenger and freight traffic in 1913, the port of entry for the great southwest. The United States Government's decision to build a great breakwater 9250 feet long, at San Pedro, against stiff opposition from commercial interests at Santa Monica and Redondo Beach, provided the southland and the City of Los Angeles, which annexed San Pedro in 1909, with the greatest manmade seaport in the world. Freight traffic was the principle source of revenue, and no less than four rail companies—the Pacific Electric, Southern Pacific, San Pedro, Los Angeles and Salt Lake, and indirectly the Santa Fe—serviced the wharfage. Lumber and other forest products provided the Pacific Electric with its most lucrative trade as the port had become the number one importer in the world of that commodity. In 1910, the port handled 642,797,461 board feet of lumber, most of which went into building homes for the southland. That same year, 284,135 passengers, both foreign and domestic, passed through the port, carried by the fifteen large steamship companies doing business at the harbor. The Pacific Electric would dispatch special trains scheduled to meet the arrival of these incoming ships, and swiftly carry its passengers to points throughout the southland. One-way fare between San Pedro and Los Angeles was about 35 cents at the time.

ALTHOUGH PRINCIPALLY DEDICATED to the passenger transportation business, freight traffic on the Pacific Electric comprised an important source of revenue to the young but powerful company. Oranges and strawberries, wire and rope, live chickens and dried meat, in less than carload quantities, along with other freight and general merchandise were brought in for local and national distribution at the Pacific Electric freight depot located at 8th Street and Hooper Avenue. U.S. Mail and express shipments, such as milk, vegetables, and other highly perishable commodities were frequently picked up en route and rushed to its ultimate destination within a few hours. Such was the case at Dominguez Junction on the Long Beach Line where fresh milk, cream, and other dairy products were loaded onto express cars and carried into the city markets for final distribution. This business and other local freight were carried on a fleet of 34 combination cars capable of hauling both passengers and freight, sometimes pulling several box cars. Carload freight for interchange service gained impetus when in 1913 the Southern Pacific and the Salt Lake railroads established through transcontinental rates. Prior to that time approximately 35 carloads a day were transferred to other carriers. Citrus traffic, mostly oranges and lemons, already keenly developed by the Santa Fe, soon found its way to the Pacific Electric and interchanged with the Southern Pacific for the line haul. The solicitation of this business was intense, the Pacific Electric laying tracks to the side and rear of packing houses already served by the Santa Fe. Shipments of petroleum products —fuel oils, asphalt, road oils, gasoline and other refined products—increased specifically as the automobile and its network of roadways expanded throughout the country. By 1916 freight business accounted for $1,867,709 or 21.6% of the company's operating revenue.

HUNTINGTON LIBRARY, SAN MARINO

HUNTINGTON LIBRARY, SAN MARINO

SPECIAL COLLECTIONS, GLENDALE PUBLIC LIBRARY

BLISS, THE END OF THE LINE on North Brand Boulevard, Glendale, the Verdugo Mountains in the background, made this a favorite weekend picnic spot for Angelinos wanting to get out to the country. A few steps away was located the well-known Casa Verdugo, a Spanish style restaurant which featured tamales, enchiladas, lemonade, and locally grown fresh fruit. L. C. Brand started a trolley line between Los Angeles and Glendale in the summer of 1903, but sold out to the Los Angeles Interurban Railway, a Huntington-Pacific Electric affiliate, who completed the project in April 1904. An opening day festival and barbeque at the Glendale Hotel on East Broadway was attended by thousands of partisan followers. A line was extended westerly into Burbank, routed along Glenoaks Boulevard, in 1911, but only after its residents had paid a bonus to the Pacific Electric for their services. As in most cases, the line opened with a huge celebration. Connections with the Glendale and Eagle Rock Railway (later the Glendale and Montrose) were made at Brand and Broadway.

AN "800" CLASS INTERURBAN RED CAR stopped to exchange passengers on Brand Boulevard at Lomita Avenue in Glendale where it was easily dwarfed by the massive eucalyptus trees, imported from Australasia, and planted years before as windbreaks for the surrounding farmland. The small triangle roofed building at the corner was a sheltered open air waiting platform, some of which were built by the local citizenry, others by the railway and sometimes by both parties. Griffith Park marks the skyline in the background.

DANNY HOWARD COLLECTION

SAFETY WAS THE RULE but not always the reality. Pacific Electric Car No. 283 met with disaster at Lamanda Park, near Walnut Street and Sierra Madre Boulevard in Pasadena, when Santa Fe Locomotive No. 1386 broadsided the car, lifted it completely off its trucks, pushed it down the line about 300 feet, and made splinters of its 36 ton wood and steel body. Usually an accident involved the Pacific Electric's high speed interurban equipment running down stray farm animals or causing a frightened horse to rear. However, less fortunate pedestrians, and drivers of horse drawn carriages and motor vehicles sometimes met their deaths as a flyer rolled along the tracks at speeds up to 70 miles per hour, hardly making a noise, and striking down unaware victims. Claims against the company were settled quickly, and a remedy was usually found to insure the nonrecurrence of the incident. The company prided itself on its safety record and developed equipment and procedures used throughout the railway industry. Perhaps its most significant development was the automatic crossing flagman or wig-wag signal which was quickly adopted by every major railway in the country.

DANNY HOWARD COLLECTION

CRAIG RASMUSSEN COLLECTION

MAINTENANCE OF WAY TOWER CAR NO. 1520 outside the 7th and Central shops in 1915 was inherited from the Los Angeles and Redondo Railway in the Great Merger. Up to 28 tower cars, whose function was to help maintain the overhead trolley wire, were used from 1911 to 1953.

FOLLOWING PAGE: BUMPER TO BUMPER TROLLEY TRAFFIC on Main Street was controlled from elevated signal towers, one of which was located on the northwest corner of Fifth and Main. Three electric railway companies—The Pacific Electric, Los Angeles Railway Company, and The Los Angeles Interurban Railway Company—all under Huntington's ownership, shared track rights on the street. The rail companies were hard pressed to keep pace with the growing demand on their lines. By 1907 the city's population was exploding, having tripled in the previous ten years to 284,000 residents. Trolley congestion was commonplace on the street where more than 2500 daily trains waited in turn to pass. Intolerable street traffic among the trains, motor vehicles and horse drawn wagons brought pressure for a solution from the irate citizenry. In 1916 The Pacific Electric proposed an extensive elevated transit system using most of the company's already existing right of way. A bond issue in 1917 to pay for the Los Angeles City and County share of grade separations, opposed by the automobile and other related interests, was defeated. Restrictions on the performance of the transit system were then affected.

H.RAPHAEL CO.
H.RAPHAEL CO.
OWL CIGAR
NOW 5¢
PAC-COAST DISTR'S.
HOTEL ROSSLY
"THANK YOU"
LILY
CREAM
G.A.THIELE,
WALL PAPER
MOUND CITY
PAINTS and OILS
Varney & Green
STORE YOUR FURNITURE & HOUSEHOLD GOODS
WAREHOUSE CO

CALIFORNIA HISTORICAL SOCIETY/TITLE INSURANCE, LOS ANGELES

HISTORICAL COLLECTIONS, SECURITY PACIFIC NATIONAL BANK

SPECIAL OR EXTRA TRAIN MOVEMENTS were as much routine to the system as any other regularly scheduled daily train. Early specials were usually charters sponsored by wealthy businessmen attempting to promote their goods or services, mostly real estate, in the land boom days after the turn of the century. A three car train of luxurious privately owned Parlor Cars waited on Hollywood Boulevard at the Paul De Longpre estate as potential land buyers posed for the camera. The cars of this class were posh, some of which were equipped with carpeted floors, portable leathered seats, lavatories, office space, porter service, mahogany panneling, a smoking section, and all with heaters and overhead lighting. The tourist trade supported the bulk of other special services. Tours of the southland were available which included the famous Tilton's Trolley Trip, from the Pasadena orange groves and Old Mission at San Gabriel to the Pavilion, parks, and Pike at Long Beach; The Balloon Route Excursion, along the westerly coastline; Orange Empire Trolley Trip through the orange groves to Riverside; Triangle Trolley Trip, via Long Beach, the Newport Beach Line to Santa Ana, and Watts; Catalina Specials to the boat connection at the harbor; and Race Track Specials to Santa Anita.

SEVERAL RESORT FACILITIES AND TOURIST ATTRACTIONS were wholly owned and operated, at various points throughout the southland, by the Pacific Electric. Among them were the Redondo Pavilion and Bath House at Redondo Beach. On July 7, 1905, the wealthy Huntington purchased the Redondo Improvement Company, which made up 90% of the city, and four days later, acquired The Los Angeles and Redondo Railway Company which he integrated with the Pacific Electric. Two years later he built the Pavilion and Bath House luring thousands of city dwellers to the seaside via his own transit lines. The Pavilion housed a variety of stores and shops—a theater, a smoking parlor, and the Mandarin Ballroom, where up to 500 couples could dance on the beechwood floors. Benny Goodman and other name bands played the House where the music ranged from the classical concerts of Bach to the up beat jazz tempo of "My Blue Heaven" and "Bye Bye Blackbird" of the twenties. The Bath House could accommodate up to 2,000 bathers in a huge indoor, tempered salt water plunge; while other amusement concessions—a shooting gallery, tunnel of love, and roller coaster—were leased to smaller concerns.

HUNTINGTON LIBRARY, SAN MARINO

INBOUND PASSENGERS PREPARED TO BOARD PE No. 347, a Los Angeles bound car on ornate Colorado Street at Fair Oaks, in the heart of Pasadena's commercial district in 1907. After traveling east on Colorado, the car turned south on Lake Avenue, passed the Hotel Wentworth on Oak Knoll Avenue, and entered Los Angeles via the four track main line. The Hotel Wentworth, defunct for several years, was purchased by Huntington, remodeled, and reopened in 1914. Pasadena, well known for its fine hotels–The Green, The Pintoresca, Maryland and Raymond–its orange groves, and proximity to the world famous Mt. Lowe Resort, appealed to an affluent class of people, many of whom stayed to settle in the area. Heralded New Year's Day events, the Tournament of Roses parade, chariot and auto races at Tournament Park and later football games at the Rose Bowl, attracted throusands to the city. On January 1, 1903, some 12,000 riders were carried to the parade route, a one day record for the company.

CRAIG RASMUSSEN COLLECTION

ELECTRIC RAIL SERVICE to the Santa Monica–Ocean Park–Venice Beach area was inaugurated in 1896 when the first of five separate but interconnected lines was opened. Communities served en route were Hollywood, Beverly Hills, Sawtelle (Old Soldiers' Home), Vineyard, Culver City, Palms, and West Los Angeles. In 1898 a pert bicyclist wheeled past a group of inbound passengers and a two car train in the commercial district of Santa Monica. Passenger business on the lines was heavy due to the resort attractions at the beaches. The holidays–Halloween, 4th of July, and New Year's Day–auto races at Santa Monica, dog races at Venice, and swim suit contests on the beaches, attracting the largest crowds. On July 4, 1914, some 29,508 passengers rode the Venice Short Line, the quickest, most direct route to the area. Freight traffic was handled on the Air Line, the outgrowth of an early steam railroad built in 1875 to facilitate the transportation of goods arriving in Santa Monica Bay from ocean vessels.

HISTORICAL COLLECTIONS, SECURITY PACIFIC NATIONAL BANK

RAY YOUNGHANS COLLECTION

PASSENGERS HAD JUST DISEMBARKED from this three-car Catalina Flyer, amidst the sand and empty lobster traps at the wharf in San Pedro. In 1910, about the time of this photo, the Pacific Electric operated 77 trains a day, in each direction, on the two lines between Los Angeles and San Pedro. Passenger business on the lines was augmented largely by the boat connection in San Pedro with Santa Catalina Island, 23 miles off the south coast. The high speed flyer service from Los Angeles to San Pedro, via Dominguez, took 43 minutes on the 22.68 mile line with way stops at Slauson Junction, Watts, and Compton. For seabound passengers, the Banning Company, with the steamships "Cabrillo" and "Hermosa," and the Wilmington Transportation Company with its fleet of steamboats operated daily service to the "Magic Isle," Catalina. The clear, blue water channel between the mainland and the island was a fisherman's paradise, with barracuda and halibut being plentiful. However, in season albacore, bonita, mackerel, sardines, skipjack, smelt, shark, and yellowtail were available in quantity.

PLEASURE BOUND PASSENGERS aboard Pacific Electric Car No. 167 rolled across the Arroyo Seco on the Garvanza Viaduct enroute to Cawston's Ostrich Farm in South Pasadena. The bridge, almost nine hundred feet long and the highest on the system, was located just west of the farm and was built by The Pasadena and Los Angeles Electric Railway in 1895. The Pacific Electric rebuilt the bridge and standard gauged the 3′6″ roadbed between Pasadena and Los Angeles shortly after it purchased the line in 1903. The route included stops at Sycamore Grove, Highland Park, Garvanza, Cawston's Ostrich Farm, and South Pasadena. The Pacific Electric capitalized on the draw of visitors to the farm and advertised its virtues extensively. Traffic on the line was so heavy that by 1911 up to ninety-eight trains a day were run in each direction; and during the peak load, a train was run every ten minutes. The farm itself was established in 1886, and at one time maintained a herd of over five hundred birds. Dyed ostrich feathers were a highly prized dress ornament and were distributed around the world by the local firm through its outlets in the United States, Canada, and Europe. Both the rail line and farm were closed during the Great Depression of the thirties.

ARROYO SECO BRANCH, LOS ANGELES PUBLIC LIBRARY

CALIFORNIA HISTORICAL SOCIETY/TITLE INSURANCE, LOS ANGELES

A PACIFIC ELECTRIC TICKET OFFICE AND TELEGRAPH STATION was located on the southwest corner of Colorado Street and Fair Oaks Avenue in Pasadena. Information, brochures, fares and reservations were available at the office. Southbound Car No. 200 edged past a local peace officer, at that corner, as another car waited on the passing track, about 1904. Pasadena's streets were criss-crossed with local and interurban trolley lines, some of which started as horsecar lines in 1886. In 1914 city lines carried 8,011,922 passengers, using 30 all steel cars, the most modern equipment available on the system. Fare within the city cost from four to five cents per ride. Gasoline, sold as one grade at the time, cost from seven to ten cents a gallon and was dispensed from the horsecart on the left.

MT. LOWE RESORT

The Rubio Canyon, Echo Mountain, Mt. Lowe Railway and resort hotel complex was a daring and unprecedented venture in its time. Today it is still considered daring, but more than that, a landmark achievement. The resort, located north of Pasadena on the slopes of the San Gabriel Mountains, became world famous soon after its opening in 1893. Four fine hotels once operated at the same time. The trolley and cable car systems were spectacular and unmatched anywhere in the world. Professor Thaddeus Lowe, a Civil War balloonist, inventor, and socialite, and the imaginative engineer David MacPherson of Cornell University pooled their resources to put together the huge project. Both Lowe and, from 1903, the Pacific Electric spared nothing to accommodate the guests and employees who used the most modern and safest facilities available. The rail line and equipment were specially designed for use in the rugged wilderness area; and in over 40 years of operation, there was not a single recorded accident. The hotels, built of the latest design, provided the guests with every convenience possible, even rivaling the prestigious hotels of downtown Los Angeles and Pasadena.

PASADENA HISTORICAL SOCIETY

PROFESSOR THADDEUS LOWE (with the white beard) can be seen sitting on top of his Mt. Lowe Railway Pleasure Coach at Third and Broadway, Los Angeles, in 1893. Stage coach travel between Pasadena and Los Angeles was the most convenient means of transporation at the time.

AN INBOUND CAR WAITED at the Poppy Fields, glowing in the sun with the California State Flower. Mountain Junction at Lake and Mendocino in Altadena was about a mile south of the fields where the tracks, wire, and poles meandered up the slope toward Rubio Canyon. The line, about two miles long, was first built to 3′6″ gauge by Lowe in 1893, later standard gauged and through-routed to Los Angeles by the Pacific Electric in 1903.

CALIFORNIA HISTORICAL SOCIETY/TITLE INSURANCE, LOS ANGELES

HUNTINGTON LIBRARY, SAN MARINO

A MOUNT LOWE CAR traveled down the grade from Rubio Pavilion near the foot of the incline. This portion of the line was single track between Hygiea and Rubio station and operated under single track rules, that is, timetable and/or dispatcher issued train orders. The distance between the two stations was about one mile, most of it cut from the granite rock around many curves, along the side of the canyon. The pavilion housed a small hotel with excellent dining facilities, a music hall, a ballroom, and the transfer station for mountain bound passengers. Upstream in the heavily wooded canyon, boarded walkways were built to nine different waterfalls and other natural attractions. More than 2,000 Japanese lanterns illuminated the area at night. A landslide and flash flood destroyed most of the complex in February 1909. The replacement structure housed only the most essential facilities, for by that time, Ye Alpine Tavern, near Mt. Lowe was the center of activity.

PASSENGERS BOARDED AN INCLINE CAR from the loading platform at Rubio Pavilion, about 1904. An event like this called for the finest attire: long dress and hat, or suit, tie and hat. On opening day, July 4, 1893, some 400 people paid five dollars each for a ride on the Great Incline, as another thousand enthusiastic spectators looked on. There were two cars, the Echo and the Rubio, with a seating capacity of 30 each and a protruding boot or small outside platform for non-fare employees and baggage. As one car came up, the other went down as both were attached to a common endless steel cable. The cable was tested to 100 tons, but never loaded to exceed five tons and was

powered by machinery at the crest of Echo Mountain. The cars traveled at three to four miles per hour and shared a common third rail except at the passing turnout located midway on the incline. The special three-tiered car bodies were removable, leaving a flat car on which freight could be loaded, principally for the hotels Echo Mountain House and Ye Alpine Tavern. Lowe, MacPherson, and Andrew Hallidie, more popularly known for his cable car engineering in San Francisco, were chiefly responsible for the design and mechanics of the incline.

WINTHROP OWEN COLLECTION

RON RUFFULO COLLECTION

AN ATTRACTIVE COUPLE appears to be taking a short-cut along the railway right of way to the creek and falls below at picturesque Rubio Canyon. The date was about 1905.

THE GREAT CABLE INCLINE nearly 3,000 feet long carried its awe-struck passengers to the top of Echo Mountain in a breathtaking seven minute ride. Passengers were lifted from the depths of Rubio Canyon to a spectacular view of the countryside, Pacific Ocean, and ships at sea many miles away. The grade varied between 48 and 62 per cent and the rise in elevation was over 1,300 feet.

CHARLES LAWRENCE PHOTO

ECHO MOUNTAIN HOUSE, chilled by the wind and snow in an infrequent wintery display, provided elegant shelter at the top of the Great Incline at 3,500 foot Echo Summit. The Chalet, a small 12 room hotel on the left and the majestic Echo Mountain House in the center, were instantly successful upon their completion and were acclaimed as two of the finest resort hotels in the world. To the right of the hotel was the incline power house, which later supported a 3,000,000 candle power searchlight, the "casino," (which was not what the name implies, but a dance hall and trainman's dormitory), the car barn, used for the maintenance and repair of mountain cars, and a water reservoir. The impressive Echo Mountain House, well appointed with specially made furniture, wooden panelled walls and carpeted floors, contained along with its 70 sleeping rooms, a bowling alley, barber shop, billiard room, shoeshine stand, social and recreation halls, and Western Union office. Between the hotel and the power house were the tracks of the spectacular Alpine Division railway which traveled 3.6 miles up and around the mountain to Ye Alpine Tavern, located at Crystal Springs. Out of view are the Mt. Lowe Observatory and a menagerie stocked with animals native to the area.

DANNY HOWARD COLLECTION

HUNTINGTON LIBRARY, SAN MARINO

IT WAS A THRILL A MINUTE for this tavern bound car and its riders as it climbed the westerly face of rugged Las Flores Canyon. There were 18 bridges, 127 curves, the longest piece of straight track being but 227 feet long, on this, the most incredible electric mountain railway on the continent.

HUNTINGTON LIBRARY, SAN MARINO

THE LINE FEATURED many engineered and natural landmarks which included Horseshoe Curve, laid out to 120 degrees of a circle. Three elevations of right of way can be seen: the lower coming from the Devil's Slide area, the second leading to the Circular Bridge and the third heading upbound toward the photographer's position and the tavern.

CIRCULAR BRIDGE LOCATED MIDWAY between Echo Mountain and Ye Alpine Tavern, designed by Chief Engineer MacPherson, increased its elevation 12 feet, as its mountain cars traversed a complete turn-around on the almost sheer cliffs above Las Flores Canyon. Passengers were thrilled as they traveled this 252 foot long bridge, the first of its kind in the world having been built on both a curve and grade. The passing spur on the left, where an upbound car met a car going down, was the only such point on the line. The single track line was always under timetable and/or train order control by the dispatcher located at Echo Mountain during the day and between 5:00 PM and 9:00 AM the following morning, in Los Angeles. The Pacific Electric's high standard of mai[illegible]nance is well noted in the finely graded roadbed, two drainage outlets [illegible] approach on the passing siding switch.

WINTHROP OWEN PHOTO

Train's last run 8/25/84

HOBOKEN, N.J. — The country's oldest operating electric railroad line, whose quaint but sturdy cars have rolled along since Thomas A. Edison inaugurated the commuter service more than half a century ago, was cranked up for the last time Friday.

Dozens of railroad buffs, some carrying champagne, boarded the 7:30 p.m. train for the final run under the old wire that was installed 54 years ago.

RAY YOUNGHANS COLLECTION

DANNY HOWARD COLLECTION

THE FAMOUS SOUTHERN CALIFORNIA INVERSION LAYER held the fog and clouds well below the Alpine Division tracks near Circular Bridge. The Pacific Electric took advantage of this natural phenomenon and advertised "the crisp, invigorating air. . . the sweet scents of sage and pine" of the Mt. Lowe Railway and Alpine Tavern, reached only by the "Big Red Cars."

SPECTACULAR CIRCULAR BRIDGE, renowned for its engineering excellence, was more notable for its seemingly precarious alignment high above the canyons and valleys below. Mountain cars would slow or stop on the bridge to allow its riders more time to enjoy the breathtaking panoramic view from this remarkable vantage point. Echo Mountain House and its complement of buildings stretched across Echo Summit when Altadena and Pasadena were still farm land on the plane below. The ride from Alpine Tavern to Echo Summit was a powerful but powerless silent ride. Pulled by gravity, the cars could coast the entire distance between the two points. Early mountain cars sometimes rolled with the trolley pole down, using only hand brakes to slow the car's speed.

THE RAILWAY PASSED THROUGH THE TIMBERLINE at Granite Gate, on the cool back side of the mountain where large cone fir, spruce, tamarack, and several varieties of oak covered the lush mountainside. Granite Gate, cut through the sheer solid walls of Grand Canyon, provided the only practical means to extend the line up the canyon and into the tavern area. It took eight months, using every man who could be used to an advantage, to blast and pick a secure roadbed through the granite outcrop. Every single tie and pole on the Alpine Division was laid in a bed of solid granite.

HUNTINGTON LIBRARY, SAN MARINO

CHARLES SEIMS COLLECTION

NARROW GAUGE CAR NO. 30 eased through the snow just a short distance from the warmth and comfort of Alpine Tavern. When snow fell, maintenance crews were called out to shovel sand on the rails which could thus afford sufficient traction for the 15 ton passenger cars to negotiate the grade. In a severe snow storm, a car was run on the line without passengers, simply to keep the line open and clear of ice and snow. For many years the line provided the most accessible route from the city into the snow country.

SWISS STYLED YE ALPINE TAVERN, located in a dense forest of ferns and trees at the head of upper Millard's Canyon at Crystal Springs, was one of the finest resort hotels in the world. Originally built as only a temporary residence and clubhouse for Lowe and his associates, the tavern and surrounding area soon became the permanent end of the line, as financial difficulties forced Lowe to stop short of his objective, a line to and a hotel at the summit of Mt. Lowe. The country suffered a financial depression in the late 1890's and Lowe was forced to sell. Apparently the setback for Lowe held little consequence for others interested in developing and maintaining the area. An auction sale in 1897 brought out three serious bidders. The Pasadena and Mt. Lowe Railway, a new corporation, purchased the enterprise, but four years later they too, were forced to sell due to their own insolvent financial position. When the proud Echo Mountain House burned to the ground on February 5, 1900, the lack of funds prevented its rebuilding. When Huntington purchased the Pasadena and Los Angeles Electric Railway in 1902, to add to his growing collection of transit lines, the Mt. Lowe Railway came with the deal. His Pacific Electric Railway continued to operate the resort, despite several major setbacks. A windstorm and fire destroyed the Chalet and every other building on Echo Mountain on December 9, 1905, with the exception of the observatory. The Incline powerhouse and a few cottages for Pacific Electric employees were rebuilt. Meanwhile the tavern, sheltered in the hills at Crystal Springs, had maintained a steady growth, enough to warrant the addition of a large bungalow, 70 cottages, and the remodeling of the tavern itself. Almost every convenience of the city hotels were available at the tavern, For instance, bell boy service, radios, telephones, electricity in every room, hot and cold running water,

PASADENA HISTORICAL SOCIETY

private baths, and heating and cooling systems. Within the tavern was located a large fireplace, around which guests would gather for an evening conversation. Informal dances were held every afternoon and evening in the music room, and both billiards and pool were played in the game room. Outside activities included hiking or horseback riding on the many trails that radiated from the area, tennis on a cement court, croquette, and miniature golf. Even the children had a playground with swings, see-saws, and a wading pool. Gourmet food was prepared by the finest chefs available and served table d'hote or a la carte. Typical dinners included such scrumptuous entrées as fried sea bass, New York count oysters, potted ox joints, roast young duckling, roast Nevada tom turkey, and a variety of special steaks. This was served with all the suitable dressings, soups, salad, vegetables, drinks, and desserts. The price on a full course meal was usually about one dollar and served with appetizing style. A short distance from the tavern was Inspiration Point with view finders locating the cities and other points of interest in the valley below. A one man one mule railway, powered by Herbert the mule, operated from 1917 to 1935 and carried its riders between Inspiration Point and Panorama Point, with an overview of Eaton Canyon. On September 15, 1936, the tavern burned to the ground. The Great Depression of the thirties had taken its toll on attendance at the tavern, and thoughts of rebuilding the hotel were shortlived. The rail line was ravished by the Great Flood of 1938 when several trestles and part of the roadbed were washed away and destroyed. The rails and other valuable metal parts were salvaged in a World War II scrap drive. Today, the U.S. Forest Service maintains hiking trails along the route of the well-nigh incredible, but almost forgotten Mt. Lowe Railway.

DOWNTOWN LOS ANGELES

Downtown Los Angeles, the geographical, business, financial, and entertainment center of urban Southern California—truly the center of attraction for millions of people was easily reached within a few minutes on the dozen or so double tracked Pacific Electric rail lines converging in the area. Daily, for several years during the twenties, and for a similar period during World War II, several hundred thousand persons rode the "Big Red Cars," most of

THE STATELY PARAMOUNT THEATER overlooked Pacific Electric operations at the corner of Sixth and Hill Streets where Pacific Electric Car No. 1461, an express box motor, headed for the beach with U.S. Mail and LCL (less than carload) freight. The car, moments before, had left the Mail and Baggage Room at the Sixth and Main Street Station, and was routed to Beverly Hills, West Los Angeles and Ocean Park, and returned via the Santa Monica Air Line. Betty Hutton and Sonny Tufts starred in the comedy "Cross My Heart," the second feature "Rolling Home" at the 3,500 seat theater. The photo was taken in the fall of 1946.

which passed through the heart of the big city. The Pacific Electric's two largest terminals–the Sixth and Main Street Station and the Subway Terminal–were located within the circumference of this magnetic center. As a matter of necessity, convenience, pleasure, or pride, transportation on the thousands of daily trains was simply a way of life. The hustling, bustling inner city provided the draw with its high employment, shopping facilities and large department stores, and the variety of entertainment locales–highlighted by the sophisticated theater houses playing the most current motion pictures. Some individuals, couples or groups took the trip into the city simply to ride and relax or eat at their favorite restaurant or cafeteria.

RAY YOUNGHANS PHOTO

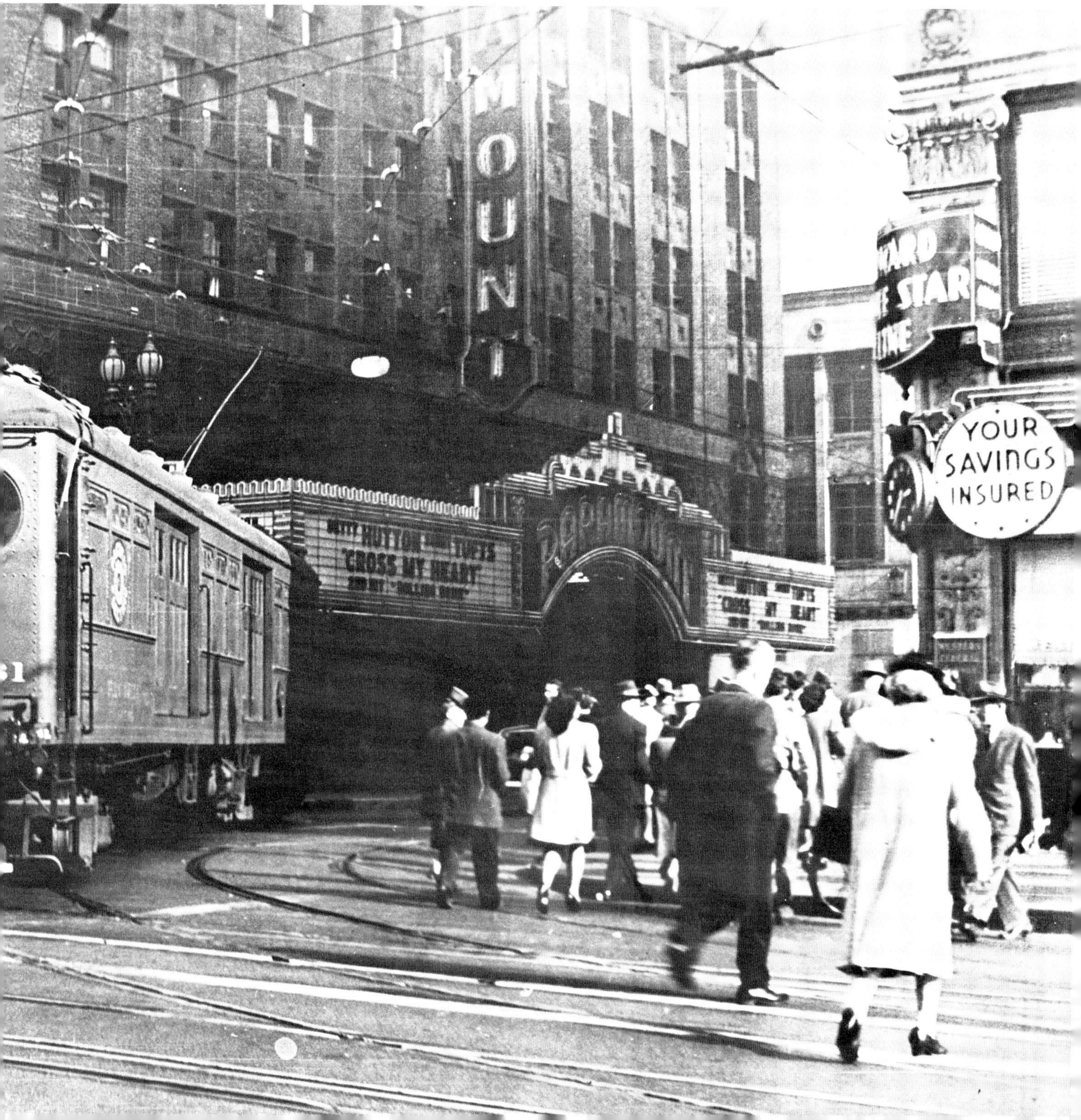

RAY YOUNGHANS COLLECTION

PACIFIC ELECTRIC CAR NO. 725 glided down the grade on Hill Street about 1948, with only light Sunday traffic to impede its speed. The car, a Hollywood-Venice Boulevard local traveled Venice Boulevard and the Sawtelle Line to its turnback point at Olympic Boulevard and Fairfax Avenue. Fares on the system were on the decline as automobiles were more popular than ever, about 1,300,000 were registered in the county at the time, a result of the post war boom. A Los Angeles Transit Lines bus was northbound at Second Street and the first of two consecutive train tunnels appeared in the background.

CHARD WALKER PHOTO

SOUTHBOUND LOS ANGELES RAILWAY "A" Line Car No. 53 passed Pacific Electric Car No. 727, a Hollywood local, at 12th and Hill Streets, September 23, 1945. The turnback for Pacific Electric Sunset Boulevard and Echo Park Avenue local cars was scarred with flange marks caused by occasional derailments.

FOLLOWING PAGE: LOS ANGELES RAILWAY CAR NO. 558 southbound at Seventh Street on Hill Street discharged passengers in front of the Warner Brothers Downtown Theater, screening George Gershwin's musical "Rhapsody in Blue." The Pacific Electric shared track rights here and on Main Street with the narrow gauge, yellow car system. The film and other downtown diversions provided temporary euphoria, diminishing crucial events incidental to World War II. The wartime photo was taken in 1942. Three autos from left to right were a 1935 Dodge, 1939 Ford, and 1938 Willys.

WARNER BROS
DOWNTOWN
THEATRE
Now Playing
Rhapsody IN BLUE
DOWNTOWN
RHAPSODY IN BLUE
WARNER BROS
RHAPSODY IN BLUE
Now PLAYING
Rhapsody IN BLUE
GO

CARL BLAUBACH PHOTO

PACIFIC ELECTRIC CAR NO. 725 EMERGED FROM THE SHADOWS on Hill Street at Ninth Street, where still another major theater, the R-K-O Hillstreet was located. Two women stood in the painted safety island, between the rail car and a 1934 Chevrolet coupe, for their protection against oncoming traffic. The rail car, a Hollywood–Los Angeles local, was but one of the designated lines using the tracks. The May Company's huge department store covered almost the entire block and rightly claimed itself "The West's Largest Store." Shoppers were especially treated at Christmas time when most of the larger department stores set up animated scenes in their display windows.

FRANK BRADFORD PHOTO

PACIFIC ELECTRIC CAR NO. 1446, A BOX MOTOR LOADED WITH FREIGHT paused for opposing traffic and pedestrians at Sixth and Hill Streets, February 18, 1947. A fenderless (no rear license plate) 1929 Ford roadster with one teardrop tail light scooted past the mammoth rail car as it headed east on Sixth Street. At the Paramount Theater, Ray Milland and Barbara Stanwyck starred in "California," a full color gold rush era movie. Except on holidays there was very little east-west traffic routed through the city. Passenger connections between the Western District and the Northern, Southern, and Eastern Districts were made on Sixth Street and once a day on the Santa Monica Air Line.

RAY YOUNGHANS PHOTO

A TWO-CAR TRAIN OF "1000" CLASS EQUIPMENT headed outbound, north of First Street on Los Angeles Street, February 23, 1944. This route among the tenement apartments and commercial buildings crossing over from Main Street to Los Angeles Street via First Street was but one of two northeasterly routes in and out of the downtown area, the other being located on San Pedro Street. United States Troops were pledged this day to protect and maintain against saboteurs, the Department of Water and Power whose employees were on a prolonged strike. In Europe, American bombers from Britain and the Mediterranean hit the Reich in their first coordinated air attack.

RAY YOUNGHANS PHOTO

RAY YOUNGHANS PHOTO

A TWO CAR TRAIN OF "1200" CLASS EQUIPMENT headed inbound Saturday, February 19, 1949, passing the Los Angeles Union Passenger Terminal, (LAUPT), at Aliso and Hewett Streets. Commuters to and from the Santa Anita Race Track in Arcadia used this route extensively, sometimes requiring several hundred trains, with as many as three cars each race day, to accommodate the traffic. A record crowd (at the track) of 53,000 jammed the grandstands and saw "Old Rockport," at 33–1 odds, upset the field and win the $100,000 Santa Anita Derby classic this day. The long shot paid $68.10, the second highest payoff in track history. Gate receipts for the day were $3,047,301.

U.S. MAIL, PARCELS, FREIGHT, fish, and fighting cocks were but a few of hundreds of commodities carried by the Pacific Electric's vast and varied fleet of express cars, also known as box motors. Pacific Electric Car No. 1405, one of four Railway Post Office (RPO) cars, departed from the Sixth and Main Street Station Mail and Baggage Dock minutes before. The car's location at Seventh and San Pedro Streets was but a short distance from its first stop at the LAUPT a few blocks away. There, a second car was added and carried outbound to San Bernardino, stopping along the way to exchange mail and freight. Inbound, a likewise operation was affected. A motorman, conductor, and two or three armed mail clerks worked the car on its trip, the clerks sorting and dispatching mail enroute. Mail was also regularly carried on passenger rail and motor coach equipment as directed by the U.S. Railway Mail Service. RPO service was discontinued July 13, 1950, the Postoffice Department favoring Highway Postoffices served by trucks.

ANDY PAYNE PHOTO

RAY YOUNGHANS PHOTO

PACIFIC ELECTRIC EXPRESS CAR NO. 1447 waited on Aliso Street at the LAUPT to couple onto an outbound RPO car, May 21, 1949. Mail and freight, loaded and unloaded at the station, were handled by Railway Express Agency employees and interchanged with the three transcontinental steam railroads using the terminal—the Santa Fe, Southern Pacific, and Union Pacific. U. S. Mail sorted, bundled, and sacked on both the steam trains and Pacific Electric RPO cars was dispatched and received directly at the stations served by the local system.

FOLLOWING PAGE: A HOTSPOT OF ENTERTAINMENT was found near the intersection of Spring, Main, and Ninth Streets where bars, burlesques, dance halls, a service man's club, and numerous movie theaters provided the climate for casual amusement. No less than seven rail lines funneled through the intersection controlled by a Los Angeles Railway signal towerman from his perch on the southeast corner (not visible). A two-car Watts local, the only scheduled Pacific Electric passenger traffic using the right of way at the time, prepared to turn east from Main to Ninth Street for its run into Watts. The Los Angeles Railway routed the "7," "8," and "N" lines along Spring Street and the "B," "F," and "O" lines on Main Street. The date was January 29, 1945.

LANE
MORTGAGE
BUILDING
LOS ANGELES
CITY CLUB
Roseland
Roof
DANCING
NIGHTLY

CHARD WALKER PHOTO

HISTORICAL COLLECTIONS, SECURITY PACIFIC NATIONAL BANK

A WESTBOUND PACIFIC ELECTRIC EDENDALE LOCAL west of Olive Street on Sixth Street was dwarfed by the large buildings lining the street. The landmark Richfield Building, with its black glazed terra cotta walls and vertical gold columns, stood at the corner of Sixth and Flower Streets in the background. The photo was taken about 1938.

HISTORICAL COLLECTIONS, SECURITY PACIFIC NATIONAL BANK

NORTHBOUND PACIFIC ELECTRIC CAR NO. 736, a "Hollywood" type car, passed southbound Los Angeles Railway Car No. 906 at Seventh and Hill Street about 1926. The Pantages Theater, later renamed the Warner Brothers, screened the Ritz Brothers in "The Marriage License" and other feature films as Rin Tin Tin in "A Hero of the Big Snows."

FRANK BRADFORD PHOTO

PACIFIC ELECTRIC CAR NO. 1356 AND CAR NO. 1359, a pair of combination cars, used for passenger, baggage, and U. S. Mail hauling, lay over at the entrance to the Los Angeles Street Yard located at the rear of the Sixth and Main Street Station. The Baggage and Mail Room, just a few yards away, was the center of U.S. Railway Mail Service activity.

TROOP TRAIN MOVEMENTS DURING WORLD WAR II were controlled by the Pacific Electric Passenger Department, at the request or order of U. S. Army Department directives. A U. S. Army Enlisting and Induction Station was located within the Sixth and Main Street Station. Volunteers and inductees, after passing required examinations, were transported to Fort MacArthur in San Pedro aboard "Extra" troop trains, which usually consisted of from three to five cars. Special troop movements included weekend and holiday trains operated between Los Angeles and San Bernardino. These were generally the largest and quickest movements on the system. From eight to twelve trains, usually consisting of five cars each, carried soldiers at speeds up to 80 miles per hour on the high speed run. Two and three car trains also operated between Los Angeles and the Santa Ana Army Air Base. The Pacific Electric, as a subcontractor to the United States Maritime Commission (U.S.M.C.), operated special "Calship" service to defense workers between Los Angeles and the Terminal Island shipyards.

RAY YOUNGHANS COLLECTION

MOTOR COACH SERVICE, used sparingly on feeder lines since 1917, further developed its use in the waning depression years when the Pacific Electric purchased 15 new yellow busses. These were placed into service July 12, 1936, on the Glendale–Burbank Line as the rail equipment in poor repair from a lack of attention underwent renovation at the Torrance Shops. The substitution, while only partial, was met with unhappy cries from those accustomed to the larger, more comfortable, and quicker rail cars. The public outcry brought about the complete restoration of rail service and the Pacific Electric accommodated its patrons by rebuilding the line and purchasing 10 new PCC type cars, the latest most modern cars to run on the system. Full service was restored November 24, 1940. Other communities and lines were affected differently. Motor coach substitutions on the Redondo via del Rey and the Santa Monica via Sawtelle lines, proved successful. Rail car speeds had been curtailed because of numerous accidents, and grade

DAVE ULLRICH COLLECTION

separations proved too costly to depreciate in the long run. Good streets and highways and the Southern California lifestyle demanded more cars and less trolleys. World War II restrictions on basic automotive supplies–gasoline, oil and rubber–temporarily stymied the use and growth of motor vehicles. The rail lines and equipment were used more than ever before. Far-sighted Pacific Electric officials, eager to keep the company operating at a profit, foresaw the eventual decline of the system as a passenger rail carrier. In 1942 a bus deck was erected at the rear of the Sixth and Main Street Station to accommodate the growing motor coach business. Rail trains were restricted from using the concourse through to Main Street except on holidays and special occasions. All passenger business, both motor coach and rail, was sold to the Metropolitan Coach Lines October 1, 1953. The photograph, a Pacific Electric publicity shot, depicted motor coach activity on the platform –every bus had been superimposed on the background print.

ERNIE LEO PHOTO

ERNIE LEO PHOTO

MILLIONS AND MILLIONS OF ANNUAL PASSENGERS passed through the gates at the Sixth and Main Street Station and into the variety of "Big Red Cars" staged to carry its bounty to hundreds of stations on the system. Passenger records were set in the early twenties, the result of spectacular growth and inflation, and again in the early forties as a result of World War II. Even in the late thirties when patronage was slowed by the Great Depression, crowds for holiday loading on the train concourse could move only en masse–that is, a group of people moved together, shoulder to shoulder, with hardly room to breathe, funneled through the gates and boarded awaiting trains as a whole. Annual statistics were astronomical. In 1926 (not a record year) 101,526,203 passengers, both revenue and free transfers, rode the rail system. There were 6,754 trains a day on the system, 3,854 of which traveled in and out of Los Angeles. The average daily car miles for an entire year, the sum total of all miles traveled by all cars per day, were 102,686, or the equivalent of one car going more than four times around the earth each day. On June 30, 1927 some 6,904 employees with an annual payroll in excess of $10,472,000, were needed to operate the system. More than 1,169 miles of single track lines were in service at the time. The impact of World War II had a marked effect upon the system as both rail and motor coach records were established. The unprecedented use of the system during this period brought with it unparalleled statistics. For three consecutive years, rail passenger traffic topped 100 million riders annually. The all time record was established in 1944 when 109,103,535 passengers took to the "Big Red Cars," and another 68,719,273 traveled on motor coaches–a grand total of 177,822,808 riders. Motor coach service peaked in 1945 when 71,001,117 passengers commuted on the buses.

PASSENGER BUSINESS OWNED BY THE METROPOLITAN COACH LINES was sold to the Los Angeles Metropolitan Transit Authority (MTA) in 1958. A two car train headed by MTA No. 1522 and outbound for Long Beach had just departed from the rear of the Sixth and Main Street Station on the elevated viaduct. An inbound Watts local, from which the photo was taken, headed for its terminus at the umbrella covered loading platform September 19, 1959. Fare to Long Beach was 73 cents on the interurban train and 15 cents from Watts to Los Angeles on the local.

CHARLES SEIMS PHOTO

ANDY PAYNE PHOTO

PACIFIC ELECTRIC CAR NO. 1217 AND TRAIN stopped at the foot of the elevated viaduct at San Pedro Street, November 18, 1948. Newspapers were picked up at this point and distributed by express and passenger cars along the line. The "Times," "Examiner," "Evening Herald and Express," "Daily News," and "Evening News" were among those carried by the system. Main line switch points within the Los Angeles Terminal District were usually automatic; however, at this important junction, which separated the Northern and Southern Districts, a large manual hand lever located inside the switch tender shanty operated the points.

THE SUBWAY

The Pacific Electric Subway, a landmark in southland transportation history, being the first and only such tunnel to date, opened November 30, 1925, and performed exceptional service until closed June 19, 1955. Built to a length of a little more than one mile, local residents took pride in the fact that the subway was the only one of its kind on the entire west coast. A ride in the tunnel, built under Bunker Hill and several major city streets, was considered a frightening experience when first opened. Prior to its use, trains routed along the heavily trafficked downtown streets were required to compete for what space was available with motorized vehicular traffic. The subway provided the necessary outlet, saving approximately eight minutes of travel time and prevented an untold number of accidents and claims.

RAY YOUNGHANS COLLECTION

PRECEDING PAGE: THE SUBWAY TERMINAL BUILDING, stately, and the city's most prestigious office building for years, contained 1,100 rooms in 250,000 square feet of floor space. The unique five winged structure with all office space open to natural sunlight crowned the subways downtown terminus. The Subway Terminal Corporation, a privately held company, owned the property and building, the Pacific Electric retaining the perpetual right to use the rail terminal and its accesses. Adjacent to the south side of the building were the surface tracks and yard for west beach trains, and above a parking lot and bus deck for supplemental motorized traffic. Inside, long, sweeping ramps were provided between the mezzanine concourse and waiting room and the six loading platforms located at trackside. Upon termination of railway operations by Metropolitan Coach Lines, the last being the Glendale Line, it was found that the Pacific Electric had defaulted on its contract. The Subway Terminal Corporation sued and the Pacific Electric agreed to remodel a small portion of the building and provide new tennants for the vacated space.

ROBERT PETERSEN PHOTO

TOWER OPERATOR C. A. BRADLEY controlled the flow of subway traffic from his perch above the tunnel throat, September 20, 1953. Three operators worked in shifts around the clock to handle the heavy flow of trains. A different train every 25 seconds could be allowed to pass through the tunnel which was also protected by automatic block signals and train stops. Should the tower operator make a single error, it was estimated that it would take between 30 to 60 minutes to rectify the mistake.

MARK EFFLE COLLECTION

RAY "SUNSHINE" EASTMAN, a ticket clerk, smiled through the open window of Pacific Electric Car No. 5012, a modern PCC class, full of outbound wartime traffic.

FOLLOWING PAGE: **THE THROAT AND FIVE TRACK TERMINAL** of the subway, four stories under Olive Street, kept railway personnel busy at all times. At the peak of operations during World War II a daily average of 754 trains and perhaps another 100 empty cars, held over at Toluca Yard for switching purposes, were routed through the tunnel. Including trains using the Hill Street surface yard, a daily total of 884 trains, consisting of 1,194 cars, entered and left the Subway Terminal in early 1944. As many as 700 trainmen and operators were supervised from the building. Numerical lights mounted on the face of the terminal control tower indicated the switch alignment and track reserved for an inbound train. Up to 30 cars could use the stub end terminal tracks at any given time. In an emergency the tower operator would sound a long blast on the tower horn: two short blasts signaled to proceed as usual. In the 30 years of subway operation there were no accidents of any consequence.

CRAIG RASMUSSEN COLLECTION

CRAIG RASMUSSEN COLLECTION

TOLUCA YARD AND SUBSTATION at the northern exit of the subway tunnel was located at the intersection of Glendale and Beverly Boulevards. The storage yard contained five holding tracks, with a capacity for 22 cars mostly held in storage for the rush hour traffic, an inspection pit and other maintenance facilities. The fully automatic substation provided most of the power requirements for the subway and terminal operations and the relocated Hill Street Station, and was interconnected with Maple Avenue, Olive and Ivanhoe Substations. Trains for Glendale–Burbank, Santa Monica–Beverly Hills via Hollywood, and the San Fernando Valley used the two track main line and subway.